# STUDY GUIDE FOR

## The Corporal and Spiritual Works of Mercy

## By Mitch Finley

# STUDY GUIDE FOR

## *The Corporal and Spiritual Works of Mercy*
## *By Mitch Finley*

## Holly Hoffman Thomas

*Foreword by Mitch Finley*

RESOURCE *Publications* • Eugene, Oregon

STUDY GUIDE FOR *THE CORPORAL AND SPIRITUAL WORKS OF MERCY* BY MITCH FINLEY

Resource Publications
An Imprint of Wipf and Stock Publishers
199 W. 8th Ave., Suite 3
Eugene, OR 97401

www.wipfandstock.com

PAPERBACK ISBN: 978-1-5326-1382-1
HARDCOVER ISBN: 978-1-5326-1384-5
EBOOK ISBN: 978-1-5326-1383-8

Manufactured in the U.S.A.                    DECEMBER 19, 2016

All Scripture References are taken from the New American Bible, Revised Edition; St. Joseph Edition, copyright 2010 by the Confraternity of Christian Doctrine, Inc., Washington, DC, U.S.A. Used by permission.

All Catechism References are from the English translation of the Catechism of the Catholic Church, Second Edition, for the United States of America, copyright 1994 by the United States Catholic Conference, Inc. Used by permission.

To *My Favorite Daddy and Rosie*
Thank you, Daddy, for being a living example of the Works of Mercy. Whether it be sheltering the homeless, giving food to the hungry, counseling the doubtful, or comforting the sorrowful, I know your heart is sincere and can feel your love radiate to all. I have enjoyed your role as BAMBI. You teach Rosie, my goddaughter and niece, as you taught me, with all the love in the world. Rosie has a heart of gold and an unbelievable imagination, always placing God first. In the span of my lifetime, you, Daddy, have taught me how to walk the walk and not just talk the talk. I love you. Forever.

To *Skyler and Baby Emma*
May you grow and learn to love the Lord following in the path of your oldest sister, Rosie. I love you so much.

# Contents

# Foreword

*Mitch Finley*

WHEN JESUS ADMONISHED HIS disciples to love God with their whole heart, mind, etc., and their neighbor as themselves, that's pretty much where the conversation ended. No one piped up with, "Um, Lord Jesus? What exactly do you mean when you say we should love our neighbor?"

In another context, however, Jesus told the story of the Good Samaritan, which nearly everyone knows about. The Samaritan—despised by the Jews of Jesus' time—loves his neighbor by caring for his physical (corporal) needs. Sacred tradition takes its cue from this by giving us the traditional Corporal and Spiritual Works of Mercy. Because we think of body and soul / corporal and spiritual as separate at our own peril, the Church offers us the works of mercy so that love of neighbor does not become a mere theory or hypothesis. Rather, to engage in the Corporal Works of Mercy is also to attend spiritual needs, as well. And to practice the Spiritual Works of Mercy is to meet others' bodily needs, too.

The more we focus on the Corporal and Spiritual Works of Mercy, the more our love for our neighbor becomes real and effective. This finely crafted study guide will give study groups, as well as individuals, what they need to better understand the Works of Mercy and put them into practice both at home and in the wider world. The more we do this, the more the world's onlookers will repeat the words of those who observed the earliest Christians: "See how they love one another."

# Acknowledgments

A SPECIAL THANKS GOES out to *Scotty*—Your constant encouragement and support of this book will never be forgotten. You are my husband and best friend. We are one.

# About the Author

HOLLY HOFFMAN THOMAS RECEIVED her Bachelor's degree in Elementary Education with a certification in Early Childhood Education and her Master's degree in Curriculum and Instruction with a certification as a Reading Specialist. She also has a minor in Religion. Holly is actively involved in her parish; leading a weekly Bible study in her home in addition to daily Mass attendance and a Holy Hour. She has an unshakable faith that remains solid. Holly's interests are in sports and music. Though Holly has no children of her own, she makes a difference in the lives of the next generation and those to come.

# Part One

## The Corporal Works of Mercy

# Chapter 1

# To Feed the Hungry

## (pages 2–10)

### Focus

WHEN WE CHOOSE TO feed the hungry, we must be authentic. The foundation of feeding the hungry is practicing the two greatest commandments: love God above all others and love your neighbor as yourself.

### Sacred Scripture

The story of the feeding of the 5000 (loaves and fishes) in ALL 4 Gospels:

#### Matthew 14:13–21

"When Jesus heard of it, he withdrew in a boat to a deserted place by himself. The crowds heard of this and followed him on foot from their towns. When he disembarked and saw the vast crowd, his heart was moved with pity for them, and he cured their sick. When it was evening, the disciples approached him and said, "This is a deserted place and it is already late; dismiss the crowds so that they can go to the villages and buy food for themselves." [Jesus] said to them, "there is no need for them to go away; give them some food yourselves." But they said to him, "Five loaves and two fish are all we have." Then he said, "Bring them here to me," and he ordered the crowds to sit down on the grass. Taking the five loaves and the two fish, and looking up to heaven, he said the blessing, broke the loaves, and gave them to the disciples, who in turn gave them to the crowds. They all ate and were satisfied, and they picked up the fragments left over—twelve wicker baskets full. Those who ate were about five thousand men, not counting women and children."

## Mark 6:32–44

"So they went off in a boat to a deserted place. People saw them leaving and many came to know about it. They hastened there on foot from all the towns and arrived at the place before them. When he disembarked and saw the vast crowd, his heart was moved with pity for them, for they were like sheep without a shepherd; and he began to teach them many things. By now it was already late and his disciples approached him and said, "This is a deserted place and it is already very late. Dismiss them so they can go to the surrounding farms and villages and buy themselves something to eat." he said to them in reply, "Give them some food yourselves." But they said to him, "Are we to buy two hundred days' wages worth of food and give it to them to eat?" He asked them, "How many loaves do you have? Go and see." And when they had found out they said, "Five loaves and two fish." So he gave orders to have them sit down in groups on the green grass. The people took their places in rows by hundreds and by fifties. Then, taking the five loaves and the two fish and looking up to heaven, he said the blessing, broke the loaves, and gave them to [his] disciples to set before the people; he also divided the two fish among them all. They all ate and were satisfied. And they picked up twelve wicker baskets full of fragments and what was left of the fish. Those who ate [of the loaves] were five thousand men."

## To Feed the Hungry

### Luke 9:10–17

"When the apostles returned, they explained to him what they had done. He took them and withdrew in private to a town called Bethsaida. The crowds, meanwhile, learned of this and followed him. He received them and spoke to them about the kingdom of God, and he healed those who needed to be cured. As the day was drawing to a close, the Twelve approached him and said, "Dismiss the crowds so they can go to the surrounding villages and farms and find lodging and provisions; for we are in a deserted place here." He said to them, "Give them some food yourselves." They replied, "Five loaves and two fish are all we have, unless we ourselves go and buy food for all these people." Now the men there numbered about five thousand. Then he said to his disciples, "Have them sit down in groups of [about] fifty." They did so and made them all sit down. Then taking the five loaves and the two fish, and looking up to heaven, he said the blessing over them, broke them, and gave them to the disciples to set before the crowd. They all ate and were satisfied. And when the leftover fragments were picked up, they filled twelve wicker baskets."

### John 6:1–13

"After this, Jesus went across the Sea of Galilee [of Tiberias]. A large crowd followed him, because they saw the signs he was performing on the sick. Jesus went up on the mountain, and there he sat down with his disciples. The Jewish feast of Passover was near. When Jesus raised his eyes and saw that a large crowd was coming to him, he said to Philip, "Where can we buy enough food for them to eat?" He said this to test him, because he himself knew what he was going to do. Philip answered him, "Two hundred days' wages worth of food would not be enough for each of them to have a little [bit]." One of the disciples, Andrew, the brother of Simon Peter, said to him, "There is a boy here who has five barley loaves and two fish; but what good are these for so many?" Jesus said, "Have the people recline." Now there was a great deal of grass in that place.

So the men reclined, about five thousand in number. Then Jesus took the loaves, gave thanks, and distributed them to those who were reclining, and also as much of the fish as they wanted. When they had had their fill, he said to his disciples, "Gather the fragments left over, so that nothing will be wasted. So they collected them, and filled twelve wicker baskets with fragments from the five barley loaves that had been more than they could eat. When the people saw the sign he had done, they said, "This is truly the Prophet, the one who is to come into the world." Since Jesus knew that they were going to come and carry him off to make him king, he withdrew again to the mountain alone."

## Catechism Connection

### Give us this day, our DAILY bread: In Brief

#2857 In the Our Father, the object of the first three petitions is the glory of the Father: the sanctification of his name, the coming of the kingdom, and the fulfillment of his will. The four others present our wants to him: they ask that our lives be nourished, healed of sin, and made victorious in the struggle of good over evil.

#2858 By asking "hallowed be thy name" we enter into God's plan, the sanctification of his name-revealed first to Moses and then in Jesus-by us and in us, in every nation and in each man.

#2859 By the second petition, the Church looks first to Christ's return and the final coming of the Reign of God. It also prays for the growth of the Kingdom of God in the "today" of our own lives.

#2860 In the third petition, we ask our Father to unite our will to that of his Son, so as to fulfill his plan of salvation in the life of the world.

#2861 In the fourth petition, by saying "give us," we express in communion with our brethren our filial trust in our heavenly

Father. "Our daily bread" refers to the earthly nourishment necessary to everyone for subsistence, and also to the Bread of Life: the Word of God and the Body of Christ. It is received in God's "today," as the indispensable, (super-) essential nourishment of the feast of the coming Kingdom anticipated in the Eucharist.

#2862 The fifth petition begs God's mercy for our offences, mercy which can penetrate our hearts only if we have learned to forgive our enemies, with the example and help of Christ.

#2863 When we say "lead us not into temptation" we are asking God not to allow us to take the path that leads to sin. This petition implores the Spirit of discernment and strength; it requests the grace of vigilance and final perseverance.

#2864 In the last petition, "but deliver us from evil," Christians pray to God with the Church to show forth the victory, already won by Christ, over the "ruler of this world," Satan, the angel personally opposed to God and to his plan of salvation.

#2865 By the final "Amen," we express our "fiat" concerning the seven petitions: "So be it."

## Service Opportunities

- Rice Bowl during Lent.
- Baby Bottle for Pro-Life (between Mother's Day and Father's Day).
- Take a meal to someone in need.
- Donate to the food pantry.
- Volunteer in a soup kitchen.

# Questions

- Compare and contrast the four Gospel accounts of the feeding of the 5000.

- Think outside the box: what are the different ways, mentioned in Chapter 1, that we, as parishioners, feed the hungry?

- How do you, as an individual, feed the hungry?

- What is one new way you can practice feeding the hungry this week?

# Chapter 2

# To Give Drink to the Thirsty

## *(pages 11–21)*

## Focus

THIRSTING FOR GOD, THE Living Water, is vital to daily living. All other "thirst" is secondary to God, who guides our life.

## Sacred Scripture

### John 4:5–14 (the woman at the well)

"He had to pass through Samaria. So he came to a town of Samaria called Sychar, near the plot of land that Jacob had given to his son Joseph. Jacob's well was there. Jesus, tired from his journey, sat down there at the well. It was about noon. A woman of Samaria came to draw water. Jesus said to her, "Give me a drink." his disciples had gone into the town to buy food. The Samaritan woman said to him, "How can you, a Jew, ask me, a Samaritan woman, for a drink?" (For Jews use nothing in common with Samaritans.) Jesus answered and said to her, "If you knew the gift of God and who is saying to you, 'Give me a drink,' you would have asked him and he would have given you living water." [The woman] said to him,

"Sir, you do not even have a bucket and the well is deep; where then can you get this living water? Are you greater than our father Jacob, who gave us this well and drank from it himself with his children and his flocks?" Jesus answered and said to her, "Everyone who drinks this water will be thirsty again; but whoever drinks the water I shall give will never thirst; the water I shall give will become in him a spring of water welling up to eternal life.'"

## Matthew 3:1–17 (John the Baptist and Jesus' baptism)

"In those days John the Baptist appeared, preaching in the desert of Judea [and] saying, "Repent, for the kingdom of heaven is at hand!" It was of him that the prophet Isaiah had spoken when he said:

> "A voice of one crying out in the desert, 'Prepare the way of the Lord, make straight his paths.'"

John wore clothing made of camel's hair and had a leather belt around his waist. His food was locusts and wild honey. At that time Jerusalem, all Judea, and the whole region around the Jordan were going out to him and were being baptized by him in the Jordan River as they acknowledged their sins. When he saw many of the Pharisees and Sadducees coming to his baptism, he said to them, "You brood of vipers! Who warned you to flee from the coming wrath? Produce good fruit as evidence of your repentance. And do not presume to say to yourselves, 'We have Abraham as our father.' For I tell you, God can raise up children to Abraham from these stones. Even now the ax lies at the root of the trees. Therefore every tree that does not bear good fruit will be cut down and thrown into the fire. I am baptizing you with water, for repentance, but the one who is coming after me is mightier than I. I am not worthy to carry his sandals. He will baptize you with the Holy Spirit and fire. His winnowing fan is in his hand. He will clear his threshing floor and gather his wheat into his barn, but the chaff he will burn with unquenchable fire." Then Jesus came from Galilee to John at the Jordan to be baptized by him. John tried to prevent him, saying, "I need to be baptized by you, and yet you are coming to me?" Jesus said to him in reply, "Allow it now, for thus it is fitting for us to fulfill all righteousness." Then he allowed him. After Jesus was baptized, he came up from the water and behold, the heavens were opened [for him], and he saw the Spirit of God descending like a dove [and] coming upon him. And a voice came from the heavens, saying, "This is my beloved Son, with whom I am well pleased."

## Catechism Connection

### Baptism: In Brief

#1275 Christian initiation is accomplished by three sacraments together: Baptism which is the beginning of new life; Confirmation which is its strengthening; and the Eucharist which nourishes the disciple with Christ's Body and Blood for his transformation in Christ.

#1276 "Go therefore and make disciples of all nations, baptizing them in the name of the Father and of the Son and of the Holy Spirit, teaching them to observe all that I have commanded you" (Mt 28:19–20).

#1277 Baptism is birth into the new life in Christ. In accordance with the Lord's will, it is necessary for salvation, as is the Church herself, which we enter by Baptism.

#1278 The essential rite of Baptism consists in immersing the candidate in water or pouring water on his head, while pronouncing the invocation of the Most Holy Trinity: the Father, the Son, and the Holy Spirit.

#1279 The fruit of Baptism, or baptismal grace, is a rich reality that includes forgiveness of original sin and all personal sins, birth into the new life by which man becomes an adoptive son of the Father, a member of Christ and a temple of the Holy Spirit. By this very fact the person baptized is incorporated into the Church, the Body of Christ, and made a sharer in the priesthood of Christ.

#1280 Baptism imprints on the soul an indelible spiritual sign, the character, which consecrates the baptized person for Christian worship. Because of the character Baptism cannot be repeated.

#1281 Those who die for the faith, those who are catechumens, and all those who, without knowing of the Church but acting under the inspiration of grace, seek God sincerely and strive to fulfill his will, can be saved even if they have not been baptized.

#1282 Since the earliest times, Baptism has been administered to children, for it is a grace and a gift of God that does not presuppose any human merit; children are baptized in the faith of the Church. Entry into Christian life gives access to true freedom.

#1283 With respect to children who have died without Baptism, the liturgy of the Church invites us to trust in God's mercy and to pray for their salvation.

#1284 In case of necessity, any person can baptize provided that he have the intention of doing that which the Church does and provided that he pours water on the candidate's head while saying: "I baptize you in the name of the Father, and of the Son, and of the Holy Spirit."

## Service Opportunities

- Water Challenge: For one 24 hour period, use no more than one gallon of water.
- Refill your water bottle instead of getting a new one each time.
- Run to the river and fill a bucket with water to use for a day.
- Go one day without using a drinking fountain.
- Invite a friend to a baptism.

# Questions

- What are some circumstances that lead you to thirst? What does it feel like when you are thirsty?

- The key to relieving thirst is finding water "fit to drink". How do you go about finding water "fit to drink"?

- How does your life relate to the Bible Story of the woman at the well?

- How does our parish/Bible Study group enrich our relationship with God and others by practicing simple acts of kindness and random acts of service?

- What is one new way you can practice giving drink to the thirsty this week?

*Chapter 3*

# To Clothe the Naked

*(pages 22–31)*

## Focus

WHILE FAITH IS CENTRAL to our belief, we still benefit from practicing the Works of Mercy.

## Sacred Scripture

Luke 3:7–16 (John the Baptist preparing the way for Jesus)

"He said to the crowds who came out to be baptized by him, "You brood of vipers! Who warned you to flee from the coming wrath? Produce good fruits as evidence of your repentance; and do not begin to say to yourselves, 'We have Abraham as our father,' for I tell you, God can raise up children to Abraham from these stones. Even now the ax lies at the root of the trees. Therefore every tree that does not produce good fruit will be cut down and thrown into the fire." And the crowds asked him, "What then should we do?" He said to them in reply, "Whoever has two tunics should share with the person who has none. And whoever has food should do likewise." Even tax collectors came to be baptized and they said to him, "Teacher, what should we do?" He answered them, "Stop collecting more than what is prescribed." Soldiers also asked him, "And what is it that we should do?" He told them, "Do not practice extortion, do not falsely accuse anyone, and be satisfied with your wages." Now the people were filled with expectation, and all were asking in their hearts whether John might be the Messiah. John answered them all, saying, "I am baptizing you with water, but one mightier than I is coming. I am not worthy to loosen the thongs of his sandals. He will baptize you with the Holy Spirit and fire."

## James 2:1–26 (Faith and Works)

"My brothers, show no partiality as you adhere to the faith in our glorious Lord Jesus Christ. For if a man with gold rings on his fingers and in fine clothes comes into your assembly, and a poor person in shabby clothes also comes in, and you pay attention to the one wearing the fine clothes and say, "Sit here, please," while you say to the poor one, "Stand there," or "Sit at my feet," have you not made distinctions among yourselves and become judges with evil designs? Listen, my beloved brothers. Did not God choose those who are poor in the world to be rich in faith and heirs of the kingdom that he promised to those who love him? But you dishonored the poor person. Are not the rich oppressing you? And do they themselves not haul you off to court? Is it not they who blaspheme the noble name that was invoked over you? However, if you fulfill the royal law according to the scripture, "You shall love your neighbor as yourself," you are doing well. But if you show partiality, you commit sin, and are convicted by the law as trans-gressors. For whoever keeps the whole law, but falls short in one particular, has become guilty in respect to all of it. For he who said, "You shall not commit adultery," also said, "You shall not kill." Even if you do not commit adultery but kill, you have become a transgressor of the law. So speak and so act as people who will be judged by the law of freedom. For the judgment is merciless to one who has not shown mercy; mercy triumphs over judgment. What good is it, my brothers, if someone says he has faith but does not have works? Can that faith save him? If a brother or sister has nothing to wear and has no food for the day, and one of you says to them, "Go in peace, keep warm, and eat well," but you do not give them the necessities of the body, what good is it? So also faith of itself, if it does not have works, is dead. Indeed someone may say, "You have faith and I have works." Demonstrate your faith to me without works, and I will demonstrate my faith to you from my works. You believe that God is one. You do well. Even the demons believe that and tremble. Do you want proof, you ignoramus, that faith without works is useless? Was not Abraham our father justified by works when he offered his son Isaac upon the altar? You see that faith was active along with his works, and faith was completed by the works. Thus the scripture was fulfilled that says, "Abraham believed God, and it was credited to him as righteousness," and he was called "the friend of God." See how a person is justified by works and not by faith alone. And in the same way, was not Rahab the harlot also justified by works when she welcomed the messengers and sent them out by a different route? For just as a body without a spirit is dead, so also faith without works is dead."

## Catechism Connection

### Believing/Faith: In Brief

#176 Faith is a personal adherence of the whole man to God who reveals himself. It involves an assent of the intellect and will to the self-revelation God has made through his deeds and words.

#177 "To believe" has thus a twofold reference: to the person, and to the truth: to the truth, by trust in the person who bears witness to it.

#178 We must believe in no one but God: the Father, the Son and the Holy Spirit.

#179 Faith is a supernatural gift from God. In order to believe, man needs the interior helps of the Holy Spirit.

#180 "Believing" is a human act, conscious and free, corresponding to the dignity of the human person.

#181 "Believing" is an ecclesial act. The Church's faith precedes, engenders, supports and nourishes our faith. The Church is the mother of all believers. "No one can have God as Father who does not have the Church as Mother" (St. Cyprian, *De unit.* 6: PL 4, 519).

#182 We believe all "that which is contained in the word of God, written or handed down, and which the Church proposes for belief as divinely revealed" (Paul VI, *CPG* # 20).

#183 Faith is necessary for salvation. The Lord himself affirms: "He who believes and is baptized will be saved; but he who does not believe will be condemned" (*Mk* 16:16).

#184 "Faith is a foretaste of the knowledge that will make us blessed in the life to come" (St. Thomas Aquinas. *Comp. theol.* 1, 2).

## Service Opportunities

- Donate clothing to desired charity.
- Knit/crochet a baby blanket for a newborn baby.
- Gently help the elderly, as they decline, get ready for the day and ready for bed.

## Questions

- Describe how parents actively practice clothing the naked on a daily basis.

## Part One: The Corporal Works of Mercy

- What is James' perspective of faith and works? What is the Catholic Church's perspective of faith and works? Do you agree or disagree with these two perspectives? Why or why not?

- This chapter goes into detail about owning more than one piece of clothing, e.g. coats. What are your thoughts about only owning one of every type of clothing you have?

- How does our parish/Bible Study group enrich our relationship with God and others by practicing clothing the naked?

- What is one new way you can practice clothing the naked this week?

# Chapter 4

# To Visit the Imprisoned

## (pages 32–41)

## Focus

THERE IS MORE TO visiting the imprisoned than solely going to the local jail or penitentiary. One must consider other types of imprisonment and listen to God about how to practice this work of mercy.

## Sacred Scripture

### Matthew 25:31–46 (the Sheep and the Goats)

"When the Son of Man comes in his glory, and all the angels with him, he will sit upon his glorious throne, and all the nations will be assembled before him. And he will separate them one from another, as a shepherd separates the sheep from the goats. He will place the sheep on his right and the goats on his left. Then the king will say to those on his right, 'Come, you who are blessed by my Father. Inherit the kingdom prepared for you from the foundation of the world. For I was hungry and you gave me food, I was thirsty and you gave me drink, a stranger and you welcomed me, naked and you clothed me, ill and you cared for me, in prison and you visited me.' Then the righteous will answer him and say, 'Lord, when did we see you hungry and feed you, or thirsty and give you drink? When did we see you a stranger and welcome you, or naked and clothe you? When did we see you ill or in prison, and visit you?' And the king will say to them in reply, 'Amen, I say to you, whatever you did for one of these least brothers of mine, you did for me.' Then he will say to those on his left, 'Depart from me, you accursed, into the eternal fire prepared for the devil and his angels. For I was hungry and you gave me no food, I was thirsty and you gave me no drink, a stranger and you gave me no welcome, naked and you gave me no clothing, ill and in prison, and you did not care for me.' Then they will answer and say, 'Lord, when did we see you hungry or thirsty or a stranger or naked or ill or in prison, and not minister to your needs?' He will answer them, 'Amen, I say to you, what you did not do for one of these least ones, you did not do for me.' And these will go off to eternal punishment, but the righteous to eternal life.'"

## Catechism Connection

## Seven Deadly Sins and our Responsibility: In Brief

#1870 "God has consigned all men to disobedience, that he may have mercy upon all" (*Rom* 11:32).

#1871 Sin is an utterance, a deed, or a desire contrary to the eternal law (St. Augustine, *Faust* 22: PL 42, 418). It is an offense against God. It rises up against God in disobedience contrary to the obedience of Christ.

#1872 Sin is an act contrary to reason. It wounds man's nature and injures human solidarity.

#1873 The root of all sins lies in man's heart. The kinds and the gravity of sins are determined principally by their objects.

#1874 To choose deliberately-that is, both knowing it and willing it-something gravely contrary to the divine law and to the ultimate end of man is to commit a mortal sin. This destroys in us the charity without which eternal beatitude is impossible. Unrepented, it brings eternal death.

#1875 Venial sin constitutes a moral disorder that is reparable by charity, which it allows to subsist in us.

#1876 The repetition of sins-even venial ones-engenders vices, among which are the capital sins.

## Freedom from Sin: In Brief

#1743 "God willed that man should be left in the hand of his own counsel (cf. *Sir* 15:14), so that he might of his own accord seek his creator and freely attain his full and blessed perfection by cleaving to him" (*GS* 17 § 1).

#1744 Freedom is the power to act or not to act, and so to perform deliberate acts of one's own. Freedom attains perfection in its acts when directed toward God, the sovereign Good.

#1745 Freedom characterizes properly human acts. It makes the human being responsible for acts of which he is the voluntary agent. His deliberate acts properly belong to him.

#1746 The imputability or responsibility for an action can be diminished or nullified by ignorance, duress, fear, and other psychological or social factors.

#1747 The right to the exercise of freedom, especially in religious and moral matters, is an inalienable requirement of the dignity of man. But the exercise of freedom does not entail the putative right to say or do anything.

#1748 "For freedom Christ has set us free" (*Gal* 5:1).

## Confession: In Brief

#1485 "On the evening of that day, the first day of the week," Jesus showed himself to his apostles. "He breathed on them, and said to them: 'Receive the Holy Spirit. If you forgive the sins of any, they are forgiven; if you retain the sins of any, they are retained'" (*Jn* 20:19, 22–23).

#1486 The forgiveness of sins committed after Baptism is conferred by a particular sacrament called the sacrament of conversion, confession, penance, or reconciliation.

#1487 The sinner wounds God's honor and love, his own human dignity as a man called to be a son of God, and the spiritual well-being of the Church, of which each Christian ought to be a living stone.

#1488 To the eyes of faith no evil is graver than sin and nothing has worse consequences for sinners themselves, for the Church, and for the whole world.

#1489 To return to communion with God after having lost it through sin is a process born of the grace of God who is rich in mercy and solicitous for the salvation of men. One must ask for this precious gift for oneself and for others.

#1490 The movement of return to God, called conversion and repentance, entails sorrow for and abhorrence of sins committed, and the firm purpose of sinning no more in the future. Conversion touches the past and the future and is nourished by hope in God's mercy.

#1491 The sacrament of Penance is a whole consisting in three actions of the penitent and the priest's absolution. The penitent's acts are repentance, confession or disclosure of sins to the priest, and the intention to make reparation and do works of reparation.

#1492 Repentance (also called contrition) must be inspired by motives that arise from faith. If repentance arises from love of charity for God, it is called "perfect" contrition; if it is founded on other motives, it is called "imperfect."

#1493 One who desires to obtain reconciliation with God and with the Church, must confess to a priest all the unconfessed grave sins he remembers after having carefully examined his conscience. The confession of venial faults, without being necessary in itself, is nevertheless strongly recommended by the Church.

#1494 The confessor proposes the performance of certain acts of "satisfaction" or "penance" to be performed by the penitent in order to repair the harm caused by sin and to re-establish habits befitting a disciple of Christ.

#1495 Only priests who have received the faculty of absolving from the authority of the Church can forgive sins in the name of Christ.

#1496 The spiritual effects of the sacrament of Penance are:

-reconciliation with God by which the penitent recovers grace;
-reconciliation with the Church;
-remission of the eternal punishment incurred by mortal sins;
-remission, at least in part, of temporal punishments resulting from sin;
-peace and serenity of conscience, and spiritual consolation;
-an increase of spiritual strength for the Christian battle.

#1497 Individual and integral confession of grave sins followed by absolution remains the only ordinary means of reconciliation with God and with the Church.

#1498 Through indulgences the faithful can obtain the remission of temporal punishment resulting from sin for themselves and also for the souls in Purgatory.

## Service Opportunities

• Volunteer in a nursing home.

• Make weekly visits to the homebound.

• Become a Eucharistic Minister in order to bring communion to the homebound, hospital, and prison.

Part One: The Corporal Works of Mercy

# Questions

- We naturally think of the imprisoned as those in jail. What are other types of imprisonment?

- List the seven deadly sins. For each of the deadly sins, name one way to break free from the imprisonment of that particular sin.

- How does our parish/Bible Study group enrich our relationship with God and others by visiting the imprisoned?

- What is one new way you can practice visiting the imprisoned this week?

# Chapter 5

# To Shelter the Homeless
## *(pages 42–51)*

## Focus

WE MUST TAKE INTO consideration that sheltering the homeless means not only to shelter physically, but also take care to of our spiritual shelter of nestling in God's arms.

## Sacred Scripture

### Matthew 10:5–15 (the Commissioning of the Disciples)

"Jesus sent out these twelve after instructing them thus, "Do not go into pagan territory or enter a Samaritan town. Go rather to the lost sheep of the house of Israel. As you go, make this proclamation: 'The kingdom of heaven is at hand.' Cure the sick, raise the dead, cleanse lepers, drive out demons. Without cost you have received; without cost you are to give. Do not take gold or silver or copper for your belts; no sack for the journey, or a second tunic, or sandals, or walking stick. The laborer deserves his keep. Whatever town or village you enter, look for a worthy person in it, and stay there until you leave. As you enter a house, wish it peace. If the house is worthy, let your peace come upon it; if not, let your peace return to you. Whoever will not receive you or listen to your words—go outside that house or town and shake the dust from your feet. Amen, I say to you, it will be more tolerable for the land of Sodom and Gomorrah on the Day of Judgment than for that town."

## Luke 9:57—62 (Jesus did not have a home)

"As they were proceeding on their journey someone said to him, "I will follow you wherever you go." Jesus answered him, "Foxes have dens and birds of the sky have nests, but the Son of Man has nowhere to rest his head." And to another he said, "Follow me." But he replied, "[Lord,] let me go first and bury my father." But he answered him, "Let the dead bury their dead. But you, go and proclaim the kingdom of God." And another said, "I will follow you, Lord, but first let me say farewell to my family at home." [To him] Jesus said, "No one who sets a hand to the plow and looks to what was left behind is fit for the kingdom of God.""

## Revelation 21:1—8 (The New Heaven and New Earth)

"Then I saw a new heaven and a new earth. The former heaven and the former earth had passed away, and the sea was no more. I also saw the holy city, a new Jerusalem, coming down out of heaven from God, prepared as a bride adorned for her husband. I heard a loud voice from the throne saying, "Behold, God's dwelling is with the human race. He will dwell with them and they will be his people and God himself will always be with them [as their God]. He will wipe every tear from their eyes, and there shall be no more death or mourning, wailing or pain, [for] the old order has passed away." The one who sat on the throne said, "Behold, I make all things new." Then he said, "Write these words down, for they are trustworthy and true." He said to me, "They are accomplished. I [am] the Alpha and the Omega, the beginning and the end. To the thirsty I will give a gift from the spring of life-giving water. The victor will inherit these gifts, and I shall be his God, and he will be my son. But as for cowards, the unfaithful, the depraved, murderers, the unchaste, sorcerers, idol-worshipers, and deceivers of every sort, their lot is in the burning pool of fire and sulfur, which is the second death.'"

## Catechism Connection

### Communion of Saints: In Brief

#960 The Church is a "communion of saints": this expression refers first to the "holy things" (sancta), above all the Eucharist, by which "the unity of believers, who form one body in Christ, is both represented and brought about" (LG 3).

#961 The term "communion of saints" refers also to the communion of "holy persons" (sancti) in Christ who "died for all," so that what each one does or suffers in and for Christ bears fruit for all.

#962 "We believe in the communion of all the faithful of Christ, those who are pilgrims on earth, the dead who are being purified, and the blessed in heaven, all together forming one Church; and we believe that in this communion, the merciful love of God and his saints is always [attentive] to our prayers" (Paul VI, CPG § 30).

## Service Opportunities

- Take in an abused victim until he/she heals enough to be on his/her own.
- Donate clothing, toiletries, etc. to a homeless shelter.
- If a Landlord, offer to let the tenants work for rent, make installments on the rent, etc.

# Questions

- What are everyday, practical ways we shelter the homeless?

- Describe how you nurture your relationship with God to stay at home in his arms.

- How would you go about leading someone to snuggle with God?

- How does our parish/Bible Study group, as the communion of saints, enrich our relationship with God and others by sheltering the homeless?

- What is one new way you can practice sheltering the homeless this week?

# Chapter 6

# To Visit the Sick
## *(pages 52–61)*

## Focus

DUE TO ORIGINAL SIN, sickness is a part of living DAILY as a Catholic Christian. We must honor God as he gives us guidelines and encouragement for when we practice this work of mercy.

## Sacred Scripture

Jesus heals the sick.

## Matthew 4:23–25

"He went around all of Galilee, teaching in their synagogues, proclaiming the gospel of the kingdom, and curing every disease and illness among the people. His fame spread to all of Syria, and they brought to him all who were sick with various diseases and racked with pain, those who were possessed, lunatics, and paralytics, and he cured them. And great crowds from Galilee, the Decapolis, Jerusalem, and Judea, and from beyond the Jordan followed him."

## Part One: The Corporal Works of Mercy

## Matthew 8:16–17

"When it was evening, they brought him many who were possessed by demons, and he drove out the spirits by a word and cured all the sick, to fulfill what had been said by Isaiah the prophet: "He took away our infirmities and bore our diseases.""

## Matthew 25:31–46

"When the Son of Man comes in his glory, and all the angels with him, he will sit upon his glorious throne, and all the nations will be assembled before him. And he will separate them one from another, as a shepherd separates the sheep from the goats. He will place the sheep on his right and the goats on his left. Then the king will say to those on his right, 'Come, you who are blessed by my Father. Inherit the kingdom prepared for you from the foundation of the world. For I was hungry and you gave me food, I was thirsty and you gave me drink, a stranger and you welcomed me, naked and you clothed me, ill and you cared for me, in prison and you visited me.' Then the righteous will answer him and say, 'Lord, when did we see you hungry and feed you, or thirsty and give you drink? When did we see you a stranger and welcome you, or naked and clothe you? When did we see you ill or in prison, and visit you?' And the king will say to them in reply, 'Amen, I say to you, whatever you did for one of these least brothers of mine, you did for me.' Then he will say to those on his left, 'Depart from me, you accursed, into the eternal fire prepared for the devil and his angels. For I was hungry and you gave me no food, I was thirsty and you gave me no drink, a stranger and you gave me no welcome, naked and you gave me no clothing, ill and in prison, and you did not care for me.' Then they will answer and say, 'Lord, when did we see you hungry or thirsty or a stranger or naked or ill or in prison, and not minister to your needs?' He will answer them, 'Amen, I say to you, what you did not do for one of these least ones, you did not do for me.' And these will go off to eternal punishment, but the righteous to eternal life."

## To Visit the Sick

### James 5:14-15

"Is anyone among you sick? He should summon the presbyters of the church, and they should pray over him and anoint [him] with oil in the name of the Lord, and the prayer of faith will save the sick person, and the Lord will raise him up. If he has committed any sins, he will be forgiven."

### 3 John 2-4

"Beloved, I hope you are prospering in every respect and are in good health, just as your soul is prospering. I rejoiced greatly when some of the brothers came and testified to how truly you walk in the truth. Nothing gives me greater joy than to hear that my children are walking in the truth."

## Catechism Connection

### Anointing of the Sick: In Brief

#1526 "Is any among you sick? Let him call for the presbyters of the Church, and let them pray over him, anointing him with oil in the name of the Lord; and the prayer of faith will save the sick man, and the Lord will raise him up; and if he has committed sins, he will be forgiven"(*Jas* 5:14-15).

#1527 The sacrament of Anointing of the Sick has as its purpose the conferral of a special grace on the Christian experiencing the difficulties inherent in the condition of grave illness or old age.

#1528 The proper time for receiving this holy anointing has certainly arrived when the believer begins to be in danger of death because of illness or old age.

#1529 Each time a Christian falls seriously ill, he may receive the Anointing of the Sick, and also when, after he has received it, the illness worsens.

Part One: The Corporal Works of Mercy

#1530 Only priests (presbyters and bishops) can give the sacrament of the Anointing of the Sick, using oil blessed by the bishop, or if necessary by the celebrating presbyter himself

#1531 The celebration of the Anointing of the Sick consists essentially in the anointing of the forehead and hands of the sick person (in the Roman Rite) or of other parts of the body (in the Eastern rite), the anointing being accompanied by the liturgical prayer of the celebrant asking for the special grace of this sacrament.

#1532 The special grace of the sacrament of the Anointing of the Sick has as its effects:

> -the uniting of the sick person to the passion of Christ, for his own good and that of the whole Church;
> -the strengthening, peace, and courage to endure in a Christian manner the sufferings of illness or old age;
> -the forgiveness of sins, if the sick person was not able to obtain it through the sacrament of Penance;
> -the restoration of health, if it is conducive to the salvation of his soul;
> -the preparation for passing over to eternal life.

## Service Opportunities

- Take a meal to a sick family member or friend.
- Volunteer in a hospital or nursing home.
- Become a Eucharistic Minister and take Communion to the homebound.
- Spend time being a companion to relieve a 24/7 caregiver of duty.

## Questions

- We tend to think of visiting the sick as tending to the physically ill. What are some other types of sicknesses?

- There are four guidelines of visiting the sick: be there, be quiet, it's not about you, and show up and shut up. Which quality is your best? Which do you feel you need to improve upon?

- As a Catholic Christian, what can you do when you discover someone is lonely?

- How does our parish/Bible Study group, as the communion of saints, enrich our relationship with God and others by visiting the sick?

- What is one new way you can practice visiting the sick this week?

*Chapter 7*

# To Bury the Dead

## *(pages 62–72)*

### Focus

AS CATHOLIC CHRISTIANS, WE are called to protect the sanctity of life from the womb to the tomb. In doing so, we fulfill God's expectation to bury the dead.

### Sacred Scripture

### Tobit 1:16–22 (courage in burying the dead)

"In the days of Shalmaneser I had performed many charitable deeds for my kindred, members of my people. I would give my bread to the hungry and clothing to the naked. If I saw one of my people who had died and been thrown behind the wall of Nineveh, I used to bury him. Sennacherib returned from Judea, having fled during the days of the judgment enacted against him by the King of heaven because of the blasphemies he had uttered; whomever he killed I buried. For in his rage he killed many Israelites, but I used to take their bodies away by stealth and bury them. So when Sennacherib looked for them, he could not find them. But a certain

34

Ninevite went and informed the king about me, that I was burying them, and I went into hiding. When I realized that the king
knew about me and that I was being hunted to be put to death, I
became afraid and took flight. All my property was confiscated; I
was left with nothing. All that I had was taken to the king's palace,
except for my wife Anna and my son Tobiah. But forty days did
not pass before two of the king's sons assassinated him and fled to
the mountains of Ararat. A son of his, Esarhaddon, succeeded him
as king. He put Ahiqar, my kinsman Anael's son, in charge of all
the credit accounts of his kingdom, and he took control over the
entire administration. Then Ahiqar interceded on my behalf, and
I returned to Nineveh. Ahiqar had been chief cupbearer, keeper of
the signet ring, treasury accountant, and credit accountant under
Sennacherib, king of the Assyrians; and Esarhaddon appointed
him as Second to himself. He was, in fact, my nephew, of my father's house, and of my own family."

## Luke 23:50—24:9 (the burial of Jesus)

"Now there was a virtuous and righteous man named Joseph who,
though he was a member of the council, had not consented to their
plan of action. He came from the Jewish town of Arimathea and
was awaiting the kingdom of God. He went to Pilate and asked for
the body of Jesus. After he had taken the body down, he wrapped
it in a linen cloth and laid him in a rock-hewn tomb in which no
one had yet been buried. It was the day of preparation, and the
sabbath was about to begin. The women who had come from Galilee with him followed behind, and when they had seen the tomb
and the way in which his body was laid in it, they returned and
prepared spices and perfumed oils. Then they rested on the sabbath according to the commandment. But at daybreak on the first
day of the week they took the spices they had prepared and went
to the tomb. They found the stone rolled away from the tomb; but
when they entered, they did not find the body of the Lord Jesus.
While they were puzzling over this, behold, two men in dazzling
garments appeared to them. They were terrified and bowed their

faces to the ground. They said to them, "Why do you seek the living one among the dead? He is not here, but he has been raised. Remember what he said to you while he was still in Galilee, that the Son of Man must be handed over to sinners and be crucified, and rise on the third day." And they remembered his words. Then they returned from the tomb and announced all these things to the eleven and to all the others."

## Catechism Connection

### Respect for the Dead: In Brief

#2318 "In [God's] hand is the life of every living thing and the breath of all mankind" (*Job* 12:10).

#2319 Every human life, from the moment of conception until death, is sacred because the human person has been willed for its own sake in the image and likeness of the living and holy God.

#2320 The murder of a human being is gravely contrary to the dignity of the person and the holiness of the Creator

#2321 The prohibition murder does not abrogate the right to render an unjust aggressor unable to inflict harm. Legitimate defense is a grave duty for whoever is responsible for the lives of others or the common good.

#2322 From its conception, the child has the right to life. Direct abortion, that is, abortion willed as an end or as a means, is a "criminal" practice (*GS* 27 § 3), gravely contrary to the moral law. The Church imposes the canonical penalty of excommunication for this crime against human life.

#2323 Because it should be treated as a person from conception, the embryo must be defended in its integrity, cared for, and healed like every other human being.

#2324 Intentional euthanasia, whatever its forms or motives, is murder. It is gravely contrary to the dignity of the human person and to the respect due to the living God, his Creator.

#2325 Suicide is seriously contrary to justice, hope, and charity. It is forbidden by the fifth commandment.

#2326 Scandal is a grave offense when by deed or omission it deliberately leads others to sin gravely.

#2327 Because of the evils and injustices that all war brings with it, we must do everything reasonably possible to avoid it. The Church prays: "From famine, pestilence, and war, O Lord, deliver us."

#2328 The Church and human reason assert the permanent validity of the moral law during armed conflicts. Practices deliberately contrary to the law of nations and to its universal principles are crimes.

#2329 "The arms race is one of the greatest curses on the human race and the harm it inflicts on the poor is more than can be endured" (*GS* 81 § 3).

#2330 "Blessed are the peacemakers, for they shall be called sons of God" (*Mt* 5:9).

## Service Opportunities

- Pray the Divine Mercy Chaplet with a sick or dying person.
- Attend funerals for family, friends, and/or fellow parishioners.
- Take a meal to a family grieving over a loved one.
- Send a card or care package to the survivors of the deceased.

# Questions

- Thinking outside the box of being physically present to bury the dead, what are other ways to practice this work of mercy?

- Describe your experience(s) with Hospice, if any at all.

- As a Catholic Christian, what can you do when someone you love is in the final stages of this earthly life?

- How does our parish/Bible Study group, as the communion of saints, enrich our relationship with God and others by burying the dead?

- What is one new way you can practice burying the dead this week?

*Part Two*

The Spiritual Works of Mercy

*Chapter 8*

# To Admonish the Sinner

## (pages 74–83)

### Focus

As Catholic Christians, we are called to live countercultural to what the world offers. When we don't, we may be culpable for our actions. That's why we should hold each other accountable to a higher standard than what the world offers.

### Sacred Scripture

Matthew 18:15–20 (when one sins against you)

"If your brother sins [against you], go and tell him his fault between you and him alone. If he listens to you, you have won over your brother. If he does not listen, take one or two others along with you, so that 'every fact may be established on the testimony of two or three witnesses.' If he refuses to listen to them, tell the church. If he refuses to listen even to the church, then treat him as you would a Gentile or a tax collector. Amen, I say to you, whatever you bind on earth shall be bound in heaven, and whatever you loose on earth shall be loosed in heaven. Again, [amen,] I say to you, if two of you agree on earth about anything for which they are to pray, it shall be granted to them by my heavenly Father. For where two or three are gathered together in my name, there am I in the midst of them."

## Thessalonians 5:12–14 (be at peace among yourselves)

"We ask you, brothers, to respect those who are laboring among you and who are over you in the Lord and who admonish you, and to show esteem for them with special love on account of their work. Be at peace among yourselves. We urge you, brothers, admonish the idle, cheer the fainthearted, support the weak, be patient with all."

## Thessalonians 3:13–15 (steer clear of those unwilling to do right)

"But you, brothers, do not be remiss in doing good. If anyone does not obey our word as expressed in this letter, take note of this person not to associate with him, that he may be put to shame. Do not regard him as an enemy but admonish him as a brother."

## Catechism Connection

### Sin: In Brief

#1870–#1876 *See study guide Chapter 4 To Visit the Imprisoned: Catechism Connection*

## Service Opportunities

- Use holy water to pray for the sinner to be released from sin.
- Pray with the sinner.
- Forgive the sinner 70 x 7 and move on.

# Questions

- Considering your personality, what words and body language would you use when admonishing the sinner? Is this how a Catholic Christian is to behave?

- Have you ever participated in an intervention? If so, what was your role and how did the intervention go in general?

- As a Catholic Christian, at what point do you need to approach someone who needs to be held culpable of his/her sins?

- How does our parish/Bible Study group, as the communion of saints, enrich our relationship with God and others by admonishing the sinner?

- What is one new way you can practice admonishing the sinner peacefully this week?

# Chapter 9

# To Instruct the Ignorant
*(pages 84–93)*

## Focus

IN THE CATHOLIC CHRISTIAN faith, ignorance refers to the absence of information. We must be open to our own learning, as learning is a life-long experience, and ready at any given moment to explain our beliefs.

## Sacred Scripture

### 1 Samuel 3:1–18 (The Lord calls Samuel)

"During the time young Samuel was minister to the LORD under Eli, the word of the LORD was scarce and vision infrequent. One day Eli was asleep in his usual place. His eyes had lately grown so weak that he could not see. The lamp of God was not yet extinguished, and Samuel was sleeping in the temple of the LORD where the ark of God was. The LORD called to Samuel, who answered, "Here I am." He ran to Eli and said, "Here I am. You called me." "I did not call you," Eli answered. "Go back to sleep." So he went back to sleep. Again the LORD called Samuel, who rose and went to Eli.

"Here I am," he said. "You called me." But he answered, "I did not call you, my son. Go back to sleep." Samuel did not yet recognize the LORD, since the word of the LORD had not yet been revealed to him. The LORD called Samuel again, for the third time. Getting up and going to Eli, he said, "Here I am. You called me." Then Eli understood that the LORD was calling the youth. So he said to Samuel, "Go to sleep, and if you are called, reply, 'Speak, LORD, for your servant is listening.'" When Samuel went to sleep in his place, the LORD came and stood there, calling out as before: Samuel, Samuel! Samuel answered, "Speak, for your servant is listening." The LORD said to Samuel: I am about to do something in Israel that will make the ears of everyone who hears it ring. On that day I will carry out against Eli everything I have said about his house, beginning to end. I announce to him that I am condemning his house once and for all, because of this crime: though he knew his sons were blaspheming God, he did not reprove them. Therefore, I swear to Eli's house: No sacrifice or offering will ever expiate its crime. Samuel then slept until morning, when he got up early and opened the doors of the temple of the LORD. He was afraid to tell Eli the vision, but Eli called to him, "Samuel, my son!" He replied, "Here I am." Then Eli asked, "What did he say to you? Hide nothing from me! May God do thus to you, and more, if you hide from me a single thing he told you." So Samuel told him everything, and held nothing back. Eli answered, "It is the LORD. What is pleasing in the LORD's sight, the LORD will do."

## Luke 2:41–52 (Jesus in the temple at age 12)

"Each year his parents went to Jerusalem for the feast of Passover, and when he was twelve years old, they went up according to festival custom. After they had completed its days, as they were returning, the boy Jesus remained behind in Jerusalem, but his parents did not know it. Thinking that he was in the caravan, they journeyed for a day and looked for him among their relatives and acquaintances, but not finding him, they returned to Jerusalem to look for him. After three days they found him in the temple, sitting in the midst of the teachers, listening to them and asking them questions, and all who heard him were astounded at his understanding and his answers. When his parents saw him, they were astonished, and his mother said to him, "Son, why have you done this to us? Your father and I have been looking for you with great anxiety." And he said to them, "Why were you looking for me? Did you not know that I must be in my Father's house? But they did not understand what he said to them. He went down with them and came to Nazareth, and was obedient to them; and his mother kept all these things in her heart. And Jesus advanced [in] wisdom and age and favor before God and man."

## Matthew 9:35–38 (like sheep without a shepherd)

"Jesus went around to all the towns and villages, teaching in their synagogues, proclaiming the gospel of the kingdom, and curing every disease and illness. At the sight of the crowds, his heart was moved with pity for them because they were troubled and abandoned, like sheep without a shepherd. Then he said to his disciples, "The harvest is abundant but the laborers are few; so ask the master of the harvest to send out laborers for his harvest."

## Catechism Connection

### Moral Conscience: In Brief

#1795 "Conscience is man's most secret core, and his sanctuary. There he is alone with God whose voice echoes in his depths".

#1796 Conscience is a judgment of reason by which the human person recognizes the moral quality of a concrete act.

#1797 For the man who has committed evil, the verdict of his conscience remains a pledge of conversion and of hope.

#1798 A well-formed conscience is upright and truthful. It formulates its judgments according to reason, in conformity with the true good willed by the wisdom of the Creator. Everyone must avail himself of the means to form his conscience.

#1799 Faced with a moral choice, conscience can make either a right judgment in accordance with reason and the divine law or, on the contrary, an erroneous judgment that departs from them.

#1800 A human being must always obey the certain judgment of his conscience.

#1801 Conscience can remain in ignorance or make erroneous judgments. Such ignorance and errors are not always free of guilt.

#1802 The Word of God is a light for our path. We must assimilate it in faith and prayer and put it into practice. This is how moral conscience is formed.

## Service Opportunities

- Brainstorm with someone to come up with ideas to use so the person can get help for him/herself.
- Study the subject together in the Bible.
- Invite to Bible Study; retreats; events.

## Questions

- How do you help others gain the knowledge to help them function in this world as a complete human being?


- Describe "preach, and if necessary, use words" as the model of instructing the ignorant.

Part Two: The Spiritual Works of Mercy

- What are your physical, emotional, mental and spiritual reactions of "choosing to do wrong" before you repent sincerely to God and the person you sinned against?

- How does our parish/Bible Study group, as the communion of saints, enrich our relationship with God and others by instructing the ignorant?

- What is one new way you can practice instructing the ignorant this week?

*Chapter 10*

# To Counsel the Doubtful

## *(pages 94–103)*

### Focus

COUNSELING THE DOUBTFUL IS not about stroking one's ego. Counseling the doubtful is all about being a sympathetic, non-judgmental listener; encouraging one to sit with questions and doubts knowing that in time God will show the way.

### Sacred Scripture

### Luke 1:26–35 (Mary says Yes to God)

"In the sixth month, the angel Gabriel was sent from God to a town of Galilee called Nazareth, to a virgin betrothed to a man named Joseph, of the house of David, and the virgin's name was Mary. And coming to her, he said, "Hail, favored one! The Lord is with you." But she was greatly troubled at what was said and pondered what sort of greeting this might be. Then the angel said to her, "Do not be afraid, Mary, for you have found favor with God. Behold, you will conceive in your womb and bear a son, and you shall name him Jesus. He will be great and will be called Son of the

Most High, and the Lord God will give him the throne of David his father, and he will rule over the house of Jacob forever, and of his kingdom there will be no end." But Mary said to the angel, "How can this be, since I have no relations with a man?" And the angel said to her in reply, "The holy Spirit will come upon you, and the power of the Most High will overshadow you. Therefore the child to be born will be called holy, the Son of God."

## Hebrews 11:1–3 (partial description of faith)

"Faith is the realization of what is hoped for and evidence of things not seen. Because of it the ancients were well attested. By faith we understand that the universe was ordered by the word of God, so that what is visible came into being through the invisible."

## Matthew 14:31 (doubt and faith are incompatible)

"Immediately Jesus stretched out his hand and caught him, and said to him, "O you of little faith, why did you doubt?""

## Matthew 21:21 (doubt and faith are incompatible)

"Jesus said to them in reply, "Amen, I say to you, if you have faith and do not waver, not only will you do what has been done to the fig tree, but even if you say to this mountain, 'Be lifted up and thrown into the sea,' it will be done.""

## Catechism Connection

### Virtues: In Brief

#1833 Virtue is a habitual and firm disposition to do good.

#1834 The human virtues are stable dispositions of the intellect and the will that govern our acts, order our passions, and guide our conduct in accordance with reason and faith. They can be grouped around the four cardinal virtues: prudence, justice, fortitude, and temperance.

#1835 Prudence disposes the practical reason to discern, in every circumstance, our true good and to choose the right means for achieving it.

#1836 Justice consists in the firm and constant will to give God and neighbor their due.

#1837 Fortitude ensures firmness in difficulties and constancy in the pursuit of the good.

#1838 Temperance moderates the attraction of the pleasures of the senses and provides balance in the use of created goods.

#1839 The moral virtues grow through education, deliberate acts, and perseverance in struggle. Divine grace purifies and elevates them.

#1840 The theological virtues dispose Christians to live in a relationship with the Holy Trinity. They have God for their origin, their motive, and their object-God known by faith, God hoped in and loved for his own sake.

#1841 There are three theological virtues: faith, hope, and charity. They inform all the moral virtues and give life to them.

#1842 By faith, we believe in God and believe all that he has revealed to us and that Holy Church proposes for our belief.

#1843 By hope we desire, and with steadfast trust await from God, eternal life and the graces to merit it.

#1844 By charity, we love God above all things and our neighbor as ourselves for love of God. Charity, the form of all the virtues, "binds everything together in perfect harmony" (*Col* 3:14).

#1845 The seven gifts of the Holy Spirit bestowed upon Christians are wisdom, understanding, counsel, fortitude, knowledge, piety, and fear of the Lord.

## Service Opportunities

- Drop everything to really listen to someone in need.
- Pray with someone who is struggling who has asked for your help.
- Be gentle and calm; offer suggestions—not "have to's".
- Be sincere when approaching and offering to help those in need.

## Questions

- Which of the three definitions of *"doubt"* do you gravitate towards when you express doubt? Why?

- Describe a time in your life when you were doubtful. Who did you turn to for help? What was said that helped/hindered you working through your doubts?

- How does our parish/Bible Study group, as the communion of saints, enrich our relationship with God and others by counseling the doubtful?

- What is one new way you can practice counseling the doubtful this week?

*Chapter 11*

# To Comfort the Sorrowful

## *(pages 104–113)*

### Focus

SORROW IS A PART of the human life. When comforting the sorrowful, we must be aware that many, many experiences lead to sorrow. We strive to be empathetic listeners. For God, and God alone is the way, the truth, and the life, and in God we place our complete trust.

### Sacred Scripture

Taking up your cross & Storing up riches in heaven.

### Matthew 16:24–25

"Then Jesus said to his disciples, "Whoever wishes to come after me must deny himself, take up his cross, and follow me. For whoever wishes to save his life will lose it, but whoever loses his life for my sake will find it.""

## Mark 8:34–35

"He summoned the crowd with his disciples and said to them, "Whoever wishes to come after me must deny himself, take up his cross, and follow me. For whoever wishes to save his life will lose it, but whoever loses his life for my sake and that of the gospel will save it.""

## Luke 14:27

"' Whoever does not carry his own cross and come after me cannot be my disciple.""

## Luke 18:18–23

"An official asked him this question, "Good teacher, what must I do to inherit eternal life?" Jesus answered him, "Why do you call me good? No one is good but God alone. You know the commandments, 'You shall not commit adultery; you shall not kill; you shall not steal; you shall not bear false witness; honor your father and your mother.'" And he replied, "All of these I have observed from my youth." When Jesus heard this he said to him, "There is still one thing left for you: sell all that you have and distribute it to the poor, and you will have a treasure in heaven. Then come, follow me." But when he heard this he became quite sad, for he was very rich."

## Catechism Connection

### Walking with God: In Brief

#2551 "Where your treasure is, there will your heart be also" (*Mt* 6:21).

#2552 The tenth commandment forbids avarice arising from a passion for riches and their attendant power.

#2553 Envy is sadness at the sight of another's goods and the immoderate desire to have them for oneself. It is a capital sin.

#2554 The baptized person combats envy through good-will, humility, and abandonment to the providence of God.

#2555 Christ's faithful "have crucified the flesh with its passions and desires" (*Gal* 5:24); they are led by the Spirit and follow his desires.

#2556 Detachment from riches is necessary for entering the Kingdom of heaven. "Blessed are the poor in spirit."

#2557 "I want to see God" expresses the true desire of man. Thirst for God is quenched by the water of eternal life (cf. *Jn* 4:14).

## Service Opportunities

- Let the hurting one guide the conversation and next steps.
- Attend services for deaths of those whom you are close to or for your friend's loved ones.
- Offer to drive so the grieving one can continue to grieve without trying to drive at the same time.
- Make time, and take time, to visit family and friends who are hurting.

## Questions

- What are your physical, emotional, mental, and spiritual reactions of feeling sorrowful?

## Part Two: The Spiritual Works of Mercy

- Describe a time in your life when you were immensely sorrowful. Who did you turn to for help? What was said that helped/hindered you working through your sorrow?



- How does our parish/Bible Study group, as the communion of saints, enrich our relationship with God and others by comforting the sorrowful?



- What is one new way you can practice comforting the sorrowful this week?

# Chapter 12

# To Bear Wrongs Patiently

## (pages 114–124)

## Focus

WHETHER ON THE GIVING or receiving end, you must learn how to bear wrongs patiently. Otherwise it can eat at you obsessively. As a Catholic Christian, the best way to practice Jesus' instructions to love one another is to continually conquer with kindness.

## Sacred Scripture

### 1 Peter 2:21–23 (trusting God to be the judge)

"For to this you have been called, because Christ also suffered for you, leaving you an example that you should follow in his footsteps.

> *"He committed no sin,*
> *and no deceit was found in his mouth."*

When he was insulted, he returned no insult; when he suffered, he did not threaten; instead, he handed himself over to the one who judges justly.

Part Two: The Spiritual Works of Mercy

## Romans 5:3–5 (purpose of our afflictions)

"Not only that, but we even boast of our afflictions, knowing that affliction produces endurance, and endurance, proven character, and proven character, hope, and hope does not disappoint, because the love of God has been poured out into our hearts through the Holy Spirit that has been given to us."

## James 5:7–12 (waiting for Jesus' 2nd coming; being nonjudgmental)

"Be patient, therefore, brothers, until the coming of the Lord. See how the farmer waits for the precious fruit of the earth, being patient with it until it receives the early and the late rains. You too must be patient. Make your hearts firm, because the coming of the Lord is at hand. Do not complain, brothers, about one another, that you may not be judged. Behold, the Judge is standing before the gates. Take as an example of hardship and patience, brothers, the prophets who spoke in the name of the Lord. Indeed we call blessed those who have persevered. You have heard of the perseverance of Job, and you have seen the purpose of the Lord, because "the Lord is compassionate and merciful." But above all, my brothers, do not swear, either by heaven or by earth or with any other oath, but let your "Yes" mean "Yes" and your "No" mean "No," that you may not incur condemnation."

## Catechism Connection

### Bearing Wrongs Patiently: In Brief

#2504 "You shall not bear false witness against your neighbor" (*Ex* 20:16). Christ's disciples have "put on the new man, created after the likeness of God in true righteousness and holiness" (*Eph* 4:24).

#2505 Truth or truthfulness is the virtue which consists in showing oneself true in deeds and truthful in words, and guarding against duplicity, dissimulation, and hypocrisy.

#2506 The Christian is not to "be ashamed of testifying to our Lord" (2 *Tim* 1:8) in deed and word. Martyrdom is the supreme witness given to the truth of the faith.

#2507 Respect for the reputation and honor of persons forbids all detraction and calumny in word or attitude.

#2508 Lying consists in saying what is false with the intention of deceiving one's neighbor.

#2509 An offense committed against the truth requires reparation.

#2510 The golden rule helps one discern, in concrete situations, whether or not it would be appropriate to reveal the truth to someone who asks for it.

#2511 "The sacramental seal is inviolable" (CIC, can. 983 # 1). Professional secrets must be kept. Confidences prejudicial to another are not to be divulged.

#2512 Society has a right to information based on truth, freedom, and justice. One should practice moderation and discipline in the use of the social communications media.

#2513 The fine arts, but above all sacred art, "of their nature are directed toward expressing in some way the infinite beauty of God in works made by human hands. Their dedication to the increase of God's praise and of his glory is more complete, the more exclusively they are devoted to turning men's minds devoutly toward God" (*SC* 122).

## Service Opportunities

- Conquer with kindness no matter what is being done to you.
- Remember it takes two to fight; so own up to your part and ask for forgiveness.
- Write out next steps to overcome what was done to you.
- Be willing to seek help, or offer assistance, for someone who is going through a tough time.

# Questions

- As Catholic Christians, we are held to a higher standard. Describe the phrases and actions you express when conquering your spouse with kindness.

- Even in a God-centered marriage, you get on each other's nerves. How can you tone down your critiques of one another so there is more time to build on each other's strengths?

- How does our parish/Bible Study group, as the communion of saints, enrich our relationship with God and others by bearing wrongs patiently?

- What is one new way you can practice bearing wrongs patiently this week?

# Chapter 13

# To Forgive All Injuries

## (pages 125–134)

### Focus

As Jesus is the ultimate example for us, God expects no less of us than to forgive ALL injuries.

### Sacred Scripture

Forgiveness through prayer is divine.

### Matthew 5:21–26

"You have heard that it was said to your ancestors, 'You shall not kill; and whoever kills will be liable to judgment.' But I say to you, whoever is angry with his brother will be liable to judgment, and whoever says to his brother, 'Raqa,' will be answerable to the Sanhedrin, and whoever says, 'You fool,' will be liable to fiery Gehenna. Therefore, if you bring your gift to the altar, and there recall that your brother has anything against you, leave your gift there at the altar, go first and be reconciled with your brother, and then come and offer your gift. Settle with your opponent quickly while on the way to court with him. Otherwise your opponent will hand you over to the judge, and the judge will hand you over to the guard, and you will be thrown into prison. Amen, I say to you, you will not be released until you have paid the last penny."

## Matthew 6:5–15

"When you pray, do not be like the hypocrites, who love to stand and pray in the synagogues and on street corners so that others may see them.

Amen, I say to you, they have received their reward. But when you pray, go to your inner room, close the door, and pray to your Father in secret. And your Father who sees in secret will repay you. In praying, do not babble like the pagans, who think that they will be heard because of their many words. Do not be like them. Your Father knows what you need before you ask him. "This is how you are to pray:

*Our Father in Heaven,*
*Hallowed be your name,*
*Your kingdom come,*
*Your will be done,*
*on earth as in heaven.*
*Give us today our daily bread;*
*and forgive us our debts,*
*as we forgive our debtors;*
*and do not subject us to the final test,*
*but deliver us from the evil one.*

If you forgive others their transgressions, your heavenly Father will forgive you. But if you do not forgive others, neither will your Father forgive your transgressions.'"

# To Forgive All Injuries

## Matthew 18:21–35

"Then Peter approaching asked him, "Lord, if my brother sins against me, how often must I forgive him? As many as seven times?" Jesus answered, "I say to you, not seven times but seventy-seven times. That is why the kingdom of heaven may be likened to a king who decided to settle accounts with his servants. When he began the accounting, a debtor was brought before him who owed him a huge amount. Since he had no way of paying it back, his master ordered him to be sold, along with his wife, his children, and all his property, in payment of the debt. At that, the servant fell down, did him homage, and said, 'Be patient with me, and I will pay you back in full.' Moved with compassion the master of that servant let him go and forgave him the loan. When that servant had left, he found one of his fellow servants who owed him a much smaller amount. He seized him and started to choke him, demanding, 'Pay back what you owe.' Falling to his knees, his fellow servant begged him, 'Be patient with me, and I will pay you back.' But he refused. Instead, he had him put in prison until he paid back the debt.

Now when his fellow servants saw what had happened, they were deeply disturbed, and went to their master and reported the whole affair. His master summoned him and said to him, 'You wicked servant! I forgave you your entire debt because you begged me to. Should you not have had pity on your fellow servant, as I had pity on you?' Then in anger his master handed him over to the torturers until he should pay back the whole debt. So will my heavenly Father do to you, unless each of you forgives his brother from his heart.'"

## Catechism Connection

### Our Father: In Brief

*#2857–#2865 See Study Guide Chapter 1 To Feed the Hungry: Catechism Connection*

## Service Opportunities

- Write a letter asking for, or giving, forgiveness.
- Go to confession regularly.
- Be willing to see both sides of the situation.

## Questions

- Describe your physical, emotional, social, and spiritual reactions when you are injured. Do your reactions change depending on the person who injured you? Why or why not?

- What is your pattern of apologizing when you have caused injury upon someone?

- How does our parish/Bible Study group, as the communion of saints, enrich our relationship with God and others by forgiving all injuries?

- What is one new way you can practice forgiving all injuries this week?

*Chapter 14*

# To Pray for the Living and the Dead

*(pages 135–144)*

## Focus

BOTH IN EARTHLY LIFE and eternal life we pray for one another. At the same time, God reigns above all and no matter our intercession on behalf of one another, God never changes his mind.

## Sacred Scripture

We, as humans, are not exempt from suffering. Suffering takes on many forms. The only way through suffering is by the power of God Almighty.

### Isaiah 53

*"Who would believe what we have heard?*
*To whom has the arm of the LORD been revealed?*
*He grew up like a sapling before him, like a shoot from the parched earth;*

*He had no majestic bearing to catch our eye, no beauty to draw us to him.*

*He was spurned and avoided by men, a man of suffering, knowing pain,*

*Like one from whom you turn your face, spurned, and we held him in no esteem.*

*Yet it was our pain that he bore, our sufferings he endured.*

*We thought of him as stricken, struck down by God and afflicted,*

*But he was pierced for our sins, crushed for our iniquity.*

*He bore the punishment that makes us whole, by his wounds we were healed.*

*We had all gone astray like sheep, all following our own way;*

*But the LORD laid upon him the guilt of us all.*

*Though harshly treated, he submitted and did not open his mouth;*

*Like a lamb led to slaughter*

> *or a sheep silent before shearers, He did not open his mouth.*

*Seized and condemned, he was taken away.*

> *Who would have thought any more of his destiny?*

*For he was cut off from the land of the living, struck for the sins of his people.*

*He was given a grave among the wicked, a burial place with evildoers,*

*Though he had done no wrong,*

> *nor was deceit found in his mouth.*

*But it was the LORD's will to crush him with pain. By making his life as a reparation offering,*

> *He shall see his offspring, shall lengthen his days,*

> *and the LORD's will shall be accomplished through him.*

*Because of his anguish he shall see the light; because of his knowledge he shall be content;*

*My servant, the just one, shall justify the many, their iniquity he shall bear.*

*Therefore I will give him his portion among the many, and he shall divide the spoils with the mighty,*

## To Pray for the Living and the Dead

*Because he surrendered himself to death, was counted among the
transgressors,*
*Bore the sins of many,*
   *and interceded for the transgressors."*

### Romans 8:26–28

"In the same way, the Spirit too comes to the aid of our weakness; for we do not know how to pray as we ought, but the Spirit itself intercedes with inexpressible groanings. And the one who searches hearts knows what the intention of the Spirit is, because it intercedes for the holy ones according to God's will. We know that all things work for good for those who love God, who are called according to his purpose."

### Luke 11:5–10

"And he said to them, "Suppose one of you has a friend to whom he goes at midnight and says, 'Friend, lend me three loaves of bread, for a friend of mine has arrived at my house from a journey and I have nothing to offer him,' and he says in reply from within, 'Do not bother me; the door has already been locked and my children and I are already in bed. I cannot get up to give you anything.' I tell you, if he does not get up to give him the loaves because of their friendship, he will get up to give him whatever he needs because of his persistence. "And I tell you, ask and you will receive; seek and you will find; knock and the door will be opened to you. For everyone who asks, receives; and the one who seeks, finds; and to the one who knocks, the door will be opened."

### 1 Timothy 2:1

"First of all, then, I ask that supplications, prayers, petitions, and thanksgivings be offered for everyone . . . "

## Romans 10:1

"Brothers, my heart's desire and prayer to God on their behalf is for salvation."

## Romans 12:14

"Bless those who persecute [you], bless and do not curse them."

## Catechism Connection

### Everlasting Life: In Brief

#1051 Every man receives his eternal recompense in his immortal soul from the moment of his death in a particular judgment by Christ, the judge of the living and the dead.

#1052 "We believe that the souls of all who die in Christ's grace . . . are the People of God beyond death. On the day of resurrection, death will be definitively conquered, when these souls will be reunited with their bodies" (Paul VI, *CPG* § 28).

#1053 "We believe that the multitude of those gathered around Jesus and Mary in Paradise forms the Church of heaven, where in eternal blessedness they see God as he is and where they are also, to various degrees, associated with the holy angels in the divine governance exercised by Christ in glory, by interceding for us and helping our weakness by their fraternal concern" (Paul VI, *CPG* § 29).

#1054 Those who die in God's grace and friendship imperfectly purified, although they are assured of their eternal salvation, undergo a purification after death, so as to achieve the holiness necessary to enter the joy of God.

#1055 By virtue of the "communion of saints," the Church commends the dead to God's mercy and offers her prayers, especially the holy sacrifice of the Eucharist, on their behalf.

#1056 Following the example of Christ, the Church warns the faithful of the "sad and lamentable reality of eternal death" (*GCD* 69), also called "hell."

#1057 Hell's principal punishment consists of eternal separation from God in whom alone man can have the life and happiness for which he was created and for which he longs.

#1058 The Church prays that no one should be lost: "Lord, let me never be parted from you." If it is true that no one can save himself, it is also true that God "desires all men to be saved" (1 *Tim* 2:4), and that for him "all things are possible" (*Mt* 19:26).

#1059 "The holy Roman Church firmly believes and confesses that on the Day of Judgment all men will appear in their own bodies before Christ's tribunal to render an account of their own deeds" (Council of Lyons II [1274]: DS 859; cf. DS 1549).

#1060 At the end of time, the Kingdom of God will come in its fullness. Then the just will reign with Christ forever, glorified in body and soul, and the material universe itself will be transformed. God will then be "all in all" (1 *Cor* 15:28), in eternal life.

# Intercessory Prayer: In Brief

#2644 The Holy Spirit who teaches the Church and recalls to her all that Jesus said also instructs her in the life of prayer, inspiring new expressions of the same basic forms of prayer: blessing, petition, intercession, thanksgiving, and praise.

#2645 Because God blesses the human heart, it can in return bless him who is the source of every blessing.

#2646 Forgiveness, the quest for the Kingdom, and every true need are objects of the prayer of petition.

#2647 Prayer of intercession consists in asking on behalf of another. It knows no boundaries and extends to one's enemies.

#2648 Every joy and suffering, every event and need can become the matter for thanksgiving which, sharing in that of Christ, should fill one's whole life: "Give thanks in all circumstances" (1 *Thess* 5:18).

#2649 Prayer of praise is entirely disinterested and rises to God, lauds him, and gives him glory for his own sake, quite beyond what he has done, but simply because HE IS.

## Service Opportunities

- Pray the Divine Mercy Chaplet as a loved one is dying.
- Fly a balloon to Heaven with a letter for whom you miss.
- Offer up your suffering for one in need.
- Become prayer partners with someone to pray for those in need.
- Commit to a Holy Hour to pray for the living and dead.

## Questions

- Describe what intercessory prayer means to you. Do you find yourself praying more for the living or dead? What saint(s) in Heaven do you ask to intercede for you?


- Have you ever prayed a NOVENA? If so, what was the purpose and end result? If not, ask your parish priest or a leader in the church for a Novena to pray and pray it with your whole heart.

## To Pray for the Living and the Dead

- How does our parish/Bible Study group, as the communion of saints, enrich our relationship with God and others by praying for the living and the dead?


- What is one new way you can practice praying for the living and the dead this week?

CPSIA information can be obtained
at www.ICGtesting.com
Printed in the USA
LVHW042200170120
644013LV00010B/743